S. G. (Samuel G.) Beatty

Beatty's guide to elegant

For self-instruction

S. G. (Samuel G.) Beatty

Beatty's guide to elegant
For self-instruction

ISBN/EAN: 9783741181030

Manufactured in Europe, USA, Canada, Australia, Japa

Cover: Foto ©Lupo / pixelio.de

Manufactured and distributed by brebook publishing software
(www.brebook.com)

S. G. (Samuel G.) Beatty

Beatty's guide to elegant

BEATTY'S GUIDE

TO

ELEGANT WRITING.

FOR SELF-INSTRUCTION

IN THE LATEST AND MOST APPROVED STYLE OF PENMANSHIP, IN FOUR PARTS, VIZ: I. COPY SLIPS; II. ORNAMENTAL SHEET; III. INSTRUCTIONS; IV. CASE.

BY S. G. BEATTY,

Principal of Ontario Commercial College.

BELLEVILLE, ONT.

THE DAILY ONTARIO STEAM PRINTING AND BOOKBINDING ESTABLISHMENT.
1876.

INTRODUCTORY REMARKS.

This series of copy-slips and book of instruction is the result of ten year's experience and close observation in the public and high schools, as well as in the largest Business College in the country. During this time penmanship, with other branches of a practical education, has received our earnest attention, having constantly under our personal supervision from fifty to two hundred students receiving instruction in this important subject; and the entire number with us during that time has been over THREE THOUSAND, varying in ages from the youth of thirteen to the man of fortyfive.

The author has, during this varied experience, had an opportunity of discovering the shoals and quicksands which wreck the pupil in penmanship, the many pitfalls which await him, and the path by which they may be avoided. The numerous applications for written copies, from friends of those who have learned penmanship with us, anxious to secure a good hand writing, and unable, on account of distance, or business engagements, to attend our institution, induced us to prepare a system for self-improvement, embracing the essential features of the regular class instruction in Ontario Commercial College.

The copies are carefully prepared and arranged in that order which the author has found to be most conducive to the rapid advancement of a student.

The soul of good penmanship is its simplicity. There are three qualities essential to fine writing—legibility, expedition and elegance; and to the attainment of these qualities this system is adapted. We endeavour to present the subject in the plainest, shortest and most interesting manner possible, without extra words or intricate unmeaning analysis, and although we have striven toward perfection in these copy-slips, we have not hoped to reach it, but trust our labor will be accepted as a faithful effort to raise the standard of this noble art and to establish a more uniform system, or universally acknowledged style of writing in Canada.

It is a matter of surprise to some, that so many of our business and professional men are poor writers. The cause of it may be attributed to the want of a plain, simple, uniform system of business penmanship, and competent instructors. While in school or college every new teacher they came under, introduced a different system, and before one was learned, another was introduced and the student asked to abandon what he had partially learned and commence in the new. The consequence of this is that to-day, among the great mass of divines, doctors, lawyers, and graduates of literary institutions, we find the most of them bad, illegible writers. Business men dash off their correspondence in such a style that it can scarcely be read. Teachers write so poorly that it seriously affects their efficiency—preventing the progress and improvement of their pupils. Ministers write their discourses so badly that it confuses them in the pulpit. Lawyers, proverbially, write so illegibly that no ordinary person can read their manuscript. Doctors write their prescriptions so badly as often to endanger the lives of their patients. Editors, whose unintelligible scrawls perplex compositors and occupy one-half their time in deciphering, often make great blunders in their editorials.

That a reform is necessary is obvious to every person giving thought to the subject ; yet how few feel themselves competent to teach penmanship as successfully as the other branches, or have as clear a conception of the subject or proper manner of presenting it as desired ! That there are radical defects, both in the present methods of instruction and the popular opinion concerning it, we are convinced; and it is the aim of this little work to correct, as well as form both taste and opinion, by establishing a standard among teachers and learners, plain, practical, and easily comprehended.

TO THE STUDENT.

Study carefully the instructions on position and movement before commencing to practice the exercises. Observe the proper style of holding the pen as shown by cuts, and the correct position for sitting at desk as given in illustrations. You have probably acquired a habit of sitting in an awkward incorrect position, holding the pen with a vice-like grasp, in a style peculiar to yourself, and writing with a cramped finger movement, and imagine it impossible to break up these habits. We assure you that it is possible for any person who has the use of the muscles of the arm to acquire a free, easy

movement, and thereby become a good penman, if he gives it sufficient application and follows our instructions.

The acquisition of an easy muscular movement is three-fourths of
the whole secret of elegant writing. It is not too much to say that
of the numerous students who have become master penman under
our supervision, not one in fifty came to us with correct habits of
position and *movement*, without which a good hand writing is impossible. We have seen the most constrained and contorted hand remod-
deled and order, freedom, symmetry and regularity evolved therefrom by adhering to the principles and properly practicing these copies
in their regular order. The first twenty-four are intended as movement exercises and should be practised over and over again, until
you acquire the proper style of holding the pen and can move the
hand readily by the action of the forearm upon its muscular rest
near the elbow. The great difficulty with the student of penmanship
is the desire to pass on to elegant writing, before position and movement are thoroughly mastered. He imagines that he must imitate
the copy as nearly as possible, from the very first, and in his attempts
to do so loses sight of the very object for which the copy is given,
and slides back into his old style of finger movement.

Persevere until you have mastered position and movement, and
always observe them, irrespective of how your writing may appear,
and practice will soon enable you to form your letters properly and
thus become a good penman.

WHAT IS GOOD WRITING?

This is an important question, and one which must be settled by
every person before he is prepared to begin the practice of penmanship to advantage. Every one has some idea, of what good writing
consists, but very few can define it, or have an idea sufficiently defi-
nite to guide their practice with any profit. Many of the failures in
attempting to acquire penmanship arise from false notions and judg-
ments of the subject. And yet there is not a subject taught in
schools and colleges that is more widely appreciated than writing,
and none upon which a judgment is passed with more freedom,
whatever may be the lack of proficiency in the judge. One is cap-
tivated by some novel or eccentric formation of a letter, and at once

pronounces the whole writing excellent. Another is enraptured with the fineness of the curved lines, and pronounces the work exquisite. A third is struck with the boldness and force of the character, and pronounces it masterly. A fourth admires the hue of the ink, and exclaims "splendid !" Thus we find almost as many different reasons for their opinions as there are individuals, because of the lack of a uniform standard of judgment and taste. No one will pronounce writing good which cannot be read, or which is slow or labored in production. The fact is, that LEGIBILITY, RAPIDITY, ADAPTATION and BEAUTY, are the requirements of good penmanship. It is the element of beauty upon which opinions and tastes usually differ. Beauty is founded upon taste, and that which appears beautiful to an uncultivated taste may appear ugly to one highly cultivated. Gaudy embellishments have ever been preferred by the uncultivated, while refined, inherent qualities, unadorned, appear most truly beautiful to the cultivated taste. Taste, like other faculties, can only be cultivated by exercise. Hence the preference of those having the most experience in writing must reasonably appear to be the most correct taste, and the best standard for determining in what the most desirable kinds of beauty exist.

CHAPTER I.

THE ESSENTIALS OF GOOD PENMANSHIP.

The essentials of good Penmanship are LEGIBILITY, RAPIDITY, ADAPTABILITY, and BEAUTY.

LEGIBILITY.

Legibility is of the first importance in penmanship. To run over a page of legible handwriting is like riding over a smooth, solid highway. To work one's way through a page of bad writing is like forcing a passage through a swamp, thick with underbrush, netted with briers, and unstable with quicksand. There is a certain honesty and friendliness in legible writing. It has a quality of justice and equity, as though it said, *I do unto others as I would they should do unto me.* Illegible writing is an incivility. It says, "What is your time, or pleasure, or convenience to me." A letter is received from a very bad writer, covering half a page of note paper which it takes over *half-an-hour* to decipher. It would have been read in less than *two minutes* if properly written. Thus there is a loss, to the recipient, of half an hour of time to say nothing of trouble and temper. The practical declaration of the writer is, "your time is of little or no importance." It is not necessary, in a time of profound peace, and on a matter of common business, to write in cypher, as though we were conspirators plotting a rebellion. Clear, well defined, legible penmanship, is like a good physiognomy in a stranger which interests us in his welfare at once. But in bad penmanship there is something unmannerly, evasive and dissembling. There are persons eminent for their talents, knowledge, and position whose handwriting is a miserable scrawl ; but all such feel deeply the neglect of this branch in their early education, and scorn the idea that "a poor handwriting is a sign of genius." There are those who, from mere snobbishness, affect to despise legibility, and who even boast that nobody can read what they write without a severe test of patience. They have heard that such and such a distinguished man wrote a miserable, tangled scrawl that nobody could read—not even the writer himself, after the ink was dry, and they seem to fancy that if they can exhibit the same ridiculous peculiarity, they establish that they too are great. This is a kind of apishness that is insipid in the extreme, not to say idiotic. It is coveting blemishes and deformities, because some great man has them. It would be just as sensible for the poetic aspirant to desire a club-foot because Lord Byron had one.

RAPIDITY.

We place rapidity next in order and importance to *legibility*. In the days of our grandfathers, before the railroad and the telegraph supplanted the stage-coach and the post-boy, a slow and labored style of writing might have suited the requirements of the time, but in the present day nothing short of an expeditious hand-writing will enable an accountant to keep pace with his work. The business writer must do his work legibly and rapidly.

To secure rapidity two things are necessary—a correct *position* and a free easy *movement*.

POSITION.—The following cut will illustrate the different positions, correct and incorrect.

CORRECT POSITION
(Side View)

Right Position.

FRONT P

INCORRECT POSITION.

(Front View)

Left Position (Standing)

POSITION.—The position chosen for writing should be a convenient one, allowing the easy action of the right hand and arm. In sitting at a desk or table there are three positions used by writers, known as the "Left-side," "Front," and "Right-side" positions. They are all practiced more or less; but it is well for the sake of order and uniformity in a class that all the pupils should observe the same position. Whichever method is adopted, those who do not wish to become hollow-chested or round-shouldered, should learn to sit easily upright, and keep the shoulders square.

The *front* and *left* positions are generally preferred by accountants and book-keepers, while the right position is used by lawyers and professional men. We prefer the front position in learning to write, and in all instances where it can be adopted, as it is the most natural and readily understood.

Sit directly in front of the desk, not touching it, nearly in an erect position—the body inclined a little forward—both feet resting on the floor in front of the chair. Steady the body with the left hand and arm, leaving the right hand and arm perfectly free for a rapid and unconstrained movement.

POSITION OF ARM.—Let the right hand rest lightly on the muscles of the forearm, near the elbow, the wrist nearly flat with the desk, and raised so that it does not touch paper or desk. The elbow should be thrown out from the body from four to six inches.

Good penmanship requires an easy, convenient, and healthful position. Many persons, however, disregard this fact, and, in many schools, a position is allowed which is detrimental, not only to good penmanship, but, if long continued, to good health also. Such a position, generally consists in crossing the legs and folding them up, in bending the back, neck, and head until they are as crooked as the famous " stick that couldn't lie still," in bringing the chin in as close proximity to the hands, as the hands are to the paper, in crooking the fingers and pinching the pen with a vice-like grasp, and, finally, in opening the mouth and making the jaws and tongue keep time to the movements of the pen and hand.

PEN HOLDING—We give below two engravings illustrating the correct position of the hand, arm and pen.

THE TWO RESTS.

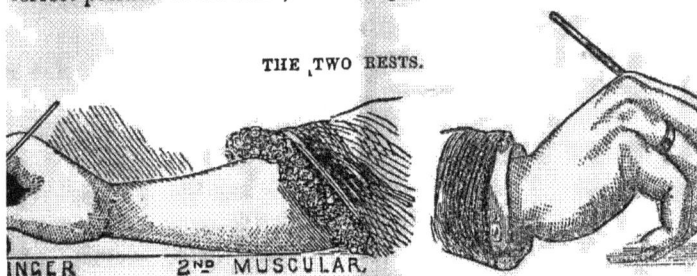

INGER   2ND MUSCULAR.

Hold the pen easily between the thumb and first two fingers. Let the first finger rest nearly on top of the holder, the end of the second finger drop below the first, so that the holder crosses it at the root of the nail and points directly towards the shoulder. The thumb should be bent a little outward, and press against the holder opposite the first finger, the holder crossing the first finger at the knuckle joint. Bend the last two fingers under, so that the hand slides on the face of the nails. The arm should rest lightly upon the edge of the desk or table, about two inches below the elbow on the fleshy part of the forearm. This constitutes the centre of motion while writing, and is so very accommodating in its elasticity as to permit the greatest freedom of movement. The wrist should *never* touch desk or paper; but the third and fourth fingers, bending gracefully under the hand, constitute a perfect moveable rest, securing the greatest accuracy of touch and steadiness of hand.

MOVEMENT.

There are three movements used in writing, the *Muscular*, the *Finger* and the *Whole-arm.* We place the Muscular movement first, because it should be first practiced in learning to write. The Muscular movement consists in the action of the forearm upon its muscular rest near the elbow; the hand gliding on the nails of the third and fourth fingers. It may be employed in making strokes in any direction. Muscular movement is specially adapted to carrying the pen rightward, and leftward, across the paper, and is most efficient in combination with the Finger movement, as will be shown. It is, however, used exclusively by some excellent penmen ; the fingers and wrist being held firmly, to check their independent action. When so used the tips of the third and fourth fingers move in lines corresponding to those produced at the point of the pen.

FINGER MOVEMENT.—This movement consists in the action of the first and second fingers and thumb, and is used chiefly in making the upward and downward strokes in loop letters. Make an l moving the fingers up and down, and in this motion you will observe the Finger Movement. It is too limited for free writing and therefore not used by good penmen.

WHOLE-ARM MOVEMENT.—This is a movement unfixed by any rest of the arm. The arm is carried above the paper, the movement coming from the shoulder, the hand resting as it always should, on the two fingers as before stated.

In striking large capitals, &c., this movement will be found valuable. It is never used for small letters, but its practice is highly beneficial as it brings into free action all the muscles from shoulder to fingers.

Long and varied experience, with careful observation, has demonstrated the fact that but two general movements are necessary in writing, namely, the combined movement and the whole-arm movement. *The Combined Movement* is the simultaneous action of the forearm, resting on the muscles, with the hand and fingers, and unites the delicate touch and stroke of the fingers with the force and freedom of the muscles. It is emphatically the business writer's movement, and enables him to execute smoothly, rapidly, and elegantly, without wearying the hand.

In order to become an elegant and ready penman, it is necessary to gain a perfect mastery of position and movement; this depends almost entirely upon the free use of the whole hand, arm and muscles. How often have you noticed this movement in the writing of some master of the pen. How rapidly he dashes off a free, beautiful business hand, as clear as print ! How graceful are the curves, and how true and bold the capitals ! And above all, with what dexterity does he ply that free movement of the hand, arm and muscles. *Position and Movement form the Philosopher's stone in Penmanship.*

Let any bad writer observe his own mode of execution, and in nine cases out of ten he will find that he bears the weight of his arm upon the wrist, and uses the last two fingers as a fixed prop. Thus his writing is uneven and crooked. How can it be otherwise? The radius of the circle of motion is very short, reaching only from the the middle finger, which is fixed, to the point of the pen. The centre of motion is changed every time he lifts his wrist, and his writing continually tends to take the form of successive segments of small circles, to prevent which he is oblidged to make constant efforts to keep on a straight line, and thus, wearies and pains his fingers. We can readily understand then, that a proper position of the pen, hand, and arm is as necessary to free, easy, rapid writing as a proper attitude of the soldier is necessary to manual dexterity in the use of his gun, on the other hand, it will be found that every elegant and ready penman has a perfect mastery of position and movement, and depends almost entirely on the use of the whole hand, arm, and muscles, and the more so in proportion to the rapidity of his execution.

ADAPTABILITY.

Penmanship should always be adapted to the circumstances under which it is used. While mathematical exactness in space, height, slope, form and shade, is admirable and essential in primary copies, to give the learner proper ideas, it is not practical under all circumstances in business writing. An accountant is often required to give explanations of entries in his books, in a limited space, and in order to accomplish it, must vary the spacing and slope of his letters accordingly. In all business writing the utmost modesty of display and simplicity of arrangement should be strictly observed. While grace lines and elaborate flourishing beautify ornamental penmanship they are as much out of place on a page of business record as a daub of oil color on a marble statue.

BEAUTY.

Under this head may properly be included FORMATION, THE PRINCIPLES, UNIFORMITY, and LIGHT and SHADE.

FORMATION.—The learner must have clear conceptions of the letters he wishes to form, before writing them. A few persons have the "imitative faculty" well developed, and can easily reproduce forms they have seen ; but others need to measure, to analyze, to describe, and to trace, before they can copy with accuracy and grace. True theory and careful persistent practice are the means by which all may learn to write, with scarcely a limit to the degree of excellence. After a good handwriting is attained, and its use becomes habitual, letters, words and sentences will flow from the ready pen, with scarcely a thought on the part of the writer as to the manner of executing them.

THE PRINCIPLES.—There are in writing two elementary characters the straight line and the curve. These two may be so combined as to form all the letters in the alphabet ; but in order to make their formation more plain, we use five principles which are given in the accompanying copy-slips. See No. V.

(1.) THE FIRST PRINCIPLE is the *convex curve,* so called because it presents the convex or rounding surface to the eye, the pen moving to the right.

(2.) THE SECOND PRINCIPLE is the *concave curve,* which is the reverse of the convex, presenting to the eye the concave or hollowing surface.

(3.) THE THIRD PRINCIPLE starts on the base-line with the convex and finishes with the concave curve.

(4.) THE FOURTH PRINCIPLE starts with the concave and finishes with the convex curve.

(5.) THE FIFTH PRINCIPLE is the oblique straight line. It holds this position in the order from the fact that it is never used in commencing a letter, and is more difficult to make than a curve. From these simple lines are formed all the letters and combinations in writing.

UNIFORMITY.

This properly includes CAPITALS, SMALL LETTERS, SLOPE, AND SPACES.

(1.) CAPITALS.—Capital letters should occupy at least three times as much space up and down as the minimum small letters. They should be of uniform size, that is, the same letters. Not that all the capitals should occupy the same space, that *I* should exactly correspond in size with *W* or *M*, but that all the *I's* and all the *M's*—all the capitals of the same kind—should agree.

An analysis of the capitals and small letters is given farther on.

¶ (2-) SMALL LETTERS.—The *small letters* consist of three classes— the *Minimum*, the *Extended Loop*, and the *Extended Stem.*

THE MINIMUM.

The minimum letter is of the smallest class, and is used as a measure for the others. This class includes

All minimum letters should correspond in length.

THE EXTENDED LOOP LETTERS ARE

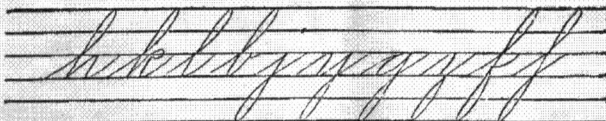

They are so called because they extend above or below the minimum letters, and are made with a loop. Extend these letters above or below the line on which you write, so as to make them just *three* spaces in height or three times the length of the minimum letters, except in ladies' hand when they should occupy *four* spaces. They should generally correspond with the length of the capitals above or below the line as the case may be.

THE EXTENDED STEM LETTERS ARE

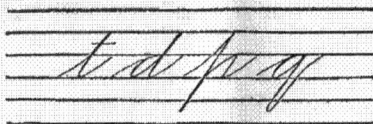

They should extend above the line of writing, twice the length of the minimum letters, *p* extends two spaces above and one and one half below the line ; *q* also one space and a half below.

SLOPE.—Most penmen prefer a slope of about fifty two degrees from the horizontal, though few agree exactly. Whatever slope is used for the first word in a manuscript, it should be followed throughout. Nothing spoils the appearance of an otherwise well-written sheet more completely than ziz-zag slopes, or indeed any departure from uniformity in this respect.

SPACING.

A SPACE is the height of the small i, which is taken as the unit of measurement for the height of small letters and capitals. In the scale of proportion we use five spaces. The contracted letters are written in the middle space, and the extended letters and capitals extend above and below. All capitals are three spaces in height; and J, Y, and Z, when brought below the line, are five. For formation of letters and spacing see slip VII. The distance between one word and another, and between letters standing for words, should be uniform. Many persons leave so little space between their words that it is almost impossible to determine where one word ends and another begins; and on the other hand some leave so much as to greatly injure the appearance of the writing.

The rule is to leave just space enough between your words to write the minimum m, to correspond in size to those used in the body of your writing.

The space between letters in a word may be given, as a general rule, to be equal to the distance between the straight lines of the letter u, and between words twice that distance.

SHADING.—Where prominence is desired, shading may be used to advantage. The contrast between light and shade, when tastefully employed, adds very much to the beauty of writing; but if improperly used, destroys it. No small letter should have more than one shade. Capitals should be shaded where it can be done the easiest, and at the same time preserve the beauty and symmetry of the letters. Shading, as a rule, is now generally omitted by the best business writers, except where prominence is desired, as it interferes with form and rapidity of execution.

Were all writing executed with heavy downward lines, as in the old-fashioned round hand, it would possess no more beauty than if the lines were uniformly light, since excess of shade as effectually destroys the contrast as its entire omission.

SMALL LETTERS.—The minimum letters are usually made without shade, though the small a, in certain combinations, sometimes receives a shade. t and d are shaded heaviest at the top, tapering gradually to the base.

The shade of p is the reverse of t, commencing near the ruled line and extending below.

In the g and q the shade is on the oval; in the b and l, on the fifth principle, base half.

Examine the copies carefully, and you will soon learn where to leave light lines and when to shade.

FIGURES.—Most business men prefer to shade each figure lightly. In the copies, we have given the best forms, all of which are shaded.

CHAPTER II.

SMALL LETTERS EXPLAINED AND ANALYZED.

The line, ruled or imaginary, upon which the letter rests is called the base line.

The horizontal line, ruled or imaginary, at the top of the short letters is sometimes called the head line; and that at the top of the capitals is called the top line.

The slant best adapted to business writing is fifty-two degrees from the horizontal.

SMALL A.

This letter is begun at the base line with a convex curve, carried up on an increased slant to the height of the letter—one space. The first downward stroke returns on this upward curve through about one-sixth of the space where it departs, in a more direct curve to the base line, and returns in the form of an oval, uniting at the top. The second downward stroke on the regular slant is brought to the base line, and the letter is finished with the upward, moving concave curve, which passes to the height of the letter. Be careful to make the turn on the base line short as before indicated. The shade on the first downward curve should be managed with care. It belongs to *minimum* class, occupies one space, and receives *one* shade.

Analysis.—Principles 1, 1, 2, 5, 2.

SMALL B.

This letter is three spaces high. It begins with an upward-moving concave curve, which turns roundly at top, and, passing down upon the regular slant, crosses the upper curve at the height of one space from the base line, forming a loop which occupies, of course, two-thirds the length of the letter. The second upstroke, which is a concave curve, is, in general direction, parallel with the down-stroke, and at the height of one space from base line, finishes with a dot and concave curve carried to the right and upward. When joined to a succeeding letter, this finishing curve takes direction accordingly. The main down-stroke is shaded from the middle to the base line. *Extended loop* class, occupies three spaces. One *shade* on down stroke near base.

Analysis.—Principles 2, 5, 2, 2, or 3, 5, 2, 2.

SMALL C.

c The small *c* is one space in height. It begins with a concave curve starting at the base line, and passing to three-fourths the height of the letter, where it joins a short down-stroke on the proper slant of writing ; this stroke is turned at the base, and with continuous curve, the line passes to the proper height of the letter and around the short down-stroke, coming down to the base line with a slight convex curve ; it turns shortly on the base line, and ends with a concave curve carried to the height of the letter. The curves on either side of the short down-stroke should be equi-distant from it, and of equal curvature. *Minimum* class. *One* space. *No shade.*

Analysis.—Principles 2, 5, 2, 1, 2.

SMALL D.

d This letter is two spaces high, formed of a pointed oval and a stem. The part measured by the first space is an exact small *a*, the only difference in the two letters being the stem part of the *d* which passes through the second space. The stem is shaded abruptly at the top, the shade gradually decreasing to the base line. Belongs to *extended stem* class.

Analysis.—Principles 1, 1, 2, 5, 2.

SMALL E.

e The small *e* occupies one space, and is very simple in its construction. It starts from the base-line with a concave curve carried well to the right, turning into a loop at the top, and coming down to the base-line with a slight convex curve ; a half-oval turn at the base, and a concave curve carried to the height of the letter, finishes it. The loop occupies three-fourths the length of the letter. *Minimum* class. *No shade.*

Analysis.—Principles 2, 1, 2—or 2, 5, 2.

SMALL F.

This letter occupies five spaces—three above and two below the base-line. It commences with a concave curve, starting at the base-line, and turning into a loop at its extreme height, where it unites with a straight line carried down on the regular inclination through the five spaces, and returning on the right with a loop-turn at bottom, joining the main down-stroke at its centre with a small entwining loop, and ending with an upward concave curve. The shade is thrown on the lower part of the main down-stroke with a gradual increase and diminution. *Extended stem* class. *One* shade.

Analysis.—Principles 2, 5, 2, 2.

SMALL G.

The first part of small *g* is formed precisely like small *a* ; the second part is carried down through three spaces, forming a loop which unites just below the base-line, the final up-curve—which is a single convex—crossing the down-stroke at that point, and continuing to the height of the letter. *Extended loop* class. *Three* spaces. *One* shade.

Analysis.—Principles 1, 1, 2, 5, 1.

SMALL H.

The small *h*, like small *b*, starts on base line with a concave curve carried up three spaces, turns at top with contracted oval or loop turn and joins a modified straight stroke, which runs directly to base-line with a gradually increasing shade ; the second part is formed of a convex curve running upward one space, joined with a half-oval turn to a downward moving straight line on the regular slant, which, at base-line, with corresponding short turn, unites with finishing concave curve, carried up one space. *Extended loop. Three* spaces. *One* shade.

Analysis.—Principles 2, 5, 1, 5, 2.

SMALL I.

This letter is the result of three simple movements, Begin on base-line with concave curve, move upward one space, return to base-line with straight stroke on regular slant, and unite, with half oval turn, to finishing concave curve, which passes upward to the height of the letter. The two curves should be parallel and equidistant from straight line at starting and finishing points. The dot, which is peculiar to this letter, should be small, and placed the distance of a space above the top of the letter in direct line of its slant. *Minimum. One space. No shade.*

Analysis.—Principles 2, 5, 2.

SMALL J.

The first part is made same as small *i* with upward concave, downward straight three spaces, upward convex or compound final. *Extended loop ; three spaces. No shade.*

Analysis.—Principles, 2, 5, 1.

SMALL K.

The first part of small *k* is formed precisely like that of small *h*, being composed of a concave or compound curve, passing from base-line upward through three spaces, turning into a loop and descending to base-line on the regular slant, with a gradually increasing shade. The second part joins the main stroke at the centre of the lower space with the convex curve, which passes a little above the height of the space, and, turning well to the right, forms a reverse oval, connecting just below the height of the space with a small up-pointing loop, thence returning to base line with the fifth principle, united by half oval turn to terminating concave curve carried up through one space. *Extended loop ; three spaces. One shade.*

Analysis.—Principles, 2, 5, 1, 2, 5, 2

SMALL L.

Upward concave or compound three spaces, downward straight to base line, upward concave final. *Extended loop ; three spaces. One shade.*

Analysis.—Principles, 2, 5, 2—or 3, 5, 2.

SMALL M.

Upward convex one space, downward straight, upward convex, downward straight, upward convex, downward straight, upward concave final. *Minimum; one space. No shade.*

Analysis.—Principles, 1, 5, 1, 5, 1, 5, 2.

SMALL N.

The small *n* has precisely the same elements and movements as the small *m*, differing only in the omission of the second part (or the second curve and second down-stroke). With this omission, the direction for forming the *m* will apply with equal force to the *n*.

SMALL O.

The small *o* occupies a single space and is a prolonged oval. The beginning and ending curves vary to suit the exigencies of the connection. For the letter, either standing alone or commencing a word, the curves are upward convex, downward convex to base line, upward concave joining at top.

Analysis.—Principles, 1, 1, 2, 2.

SMALL P.

Upward concave two spaces, downward straight three spaces, upward short convex, downward straight, upward concave final. *Extended stem*, three spaces, two above and one below base line. *One shade.*

Analysis.—Principles, 2, 5, 1, 5, 2.

SMALL Q.

This letter differs from the small *g* only in the position and form of the terminating curve. Instead of a loop formation of the extended part, as in *g*, the main down-stroke passes $1\frac{1}{2}$ spaces below the base line, and with a short turn to the right, the letter is finished with an upward convex curve, running, in the main, parallel with the down-stroke as far as the base-line, and thence more positively to the right, ending at the height of one space. The first or oval part is formed exactly like the first part of *a*, *d*, and *g*. *Extended stem ; two and a half spaces.*

Analysis.—Principles, 1, 1, 2, 5, 2, 2.

SMALL R.

The small *r* is nearly identical in movement and form with small *i*. The first up-curve (concave) is carried one-fourth of a space above the height of *i* ; from this point an almost perpendicular convex curve passes down to the top of first space, forming a sort of shoulder, and joined to a straight down-stroke on the usual slant, which turns at base line with half-oval turn, finishing with concave curve carried up through one space. *Minimum. No shade.*

    Analysis.—Principles 2, 1, 5, 2.

SMALL S.

The main difference between the capital and small *s* exists in the upper loop, which is wholly omitted in the latter. The main down-stroke of the small *s* is a compound curve, but the upper or concave portion is much shorter and less perceptible than the lower or concave. Commence on base-line with concave curve carried upward one and a fourth space; return on this curve to the height of one space, whence diverge into a more full curve, turning roundly at base-line and uniting with the first stroke just above the base-line in a small dot. Thence follow the curve back to the base-line, and finish with concave curve carried to the height of one space. *Minimum. One space. No shade.*

    Analysis.—Principles 2, 4, 2.

SMALL T.

The movements of this letter are identical with those of small *i*, the difference being in the height—*t* occupying two spaces, and *i* one. Begin on base line with concave curve, and pass upward to height of letter, two spaces; with an abrupt square shade at top, return to base-line on the regular slant, covering the upward curve through half the distance, separating therefrom at the height of one space from base-line. Turn short on base-line, and finish with concave curve carried up through one space. The shade, which commences abruptly at the top of the letter, gradually decreases to base line. The cross, which is made one half space from the top, should be light, short, and run parallel with base-line. *Extended stem; two spaces. One shade.*

    Analysis.—Principles, 2, 5, 2,

SMALL U.

Small *u* is a simple small *n* inverted. It occupies a space in height, and comprises five simple movements, as indicated in the accompanying analysis, viz., three concave curves, and two straight strokes. The principles occur in the following order : 2, 5, 2, 5, 2.

NOTE.—Observe the distance between the parts, as also the connection at top and bottom. No two lines run together ; the curves and straight lines alternate, the curves being parallel to each other and the straight lines the same.

SMALL V.

Small *v* occupies one space in height. Commence on base-line with convex curve, carry upward one space, join with half oval turn to straight down-stroke on the regular slant, turn on base-line and pass upward with concave curve through one space, ending with small dot and sagging curve carried to the right. *Minimum.* No shade.

Analysis.—Principles 1, 5, 2, 2.

SMALL W.

Upward concave one space, downward straight, upward concave, downward straight, upward concave, horizontal concave final. *Minimum. One* space.

Analysis.—Principles 2, 5, 2, 5, 2, 2.

SMALL X.

The first part of small *x* differs from the first part of *n* and *m* in the increased slant of the down-stroke, which is necessary to give the letter correct form and proper position on the line. The second part is the exact reverse of the first part, the two touching in the center. When properly formed and united, the letter has the appearance of a straight line crossing a compound curve. The distance between the two parts at top and bottom, is the same as that between the parts of *m* and *n. Minimum. One* space. *No* shade.

Analysis —Principles 1, 2, 1, 2.

SMALL Y.

Small *y* occupies three spaces—two below the base-line, and one above. It is in form exactly the reverse of small *h*, or small *h* inverted. The shade, however, is usually thrown on the contracted part, while in *h* it is located on the main portion, or stem, gradually increasing from the center to the bottom, or base-line.

Begin on base-line with convex curve ; carry upward through one space, and, with half oval turn, return to base-line ; their unite through a corresponding turn to a concave curve carried upward one space ; join with acute angle to a down-stroke on the usual slant, which passes through three spaces, turning at bottom, and with upward-moving convex curve form a graceful loop. The up-curve crosses down-stroke just below base-line, and continues to the height of the letter. *Extended loop. Three* spaces. *One* shade.

Analysis.—Principles 1, 5, 2, 5, 1.

SMALL Z.

This letter occupies three spaces, one above and two below the base-line. Commence on base-line with convex curve, carry up one space, turning at top with a round turn ; continue to base-line with an increasing slope, forming thereon a small loop ; continue downward through two spaces, and with a leftward loop-turn at bottom pass up on a slight convex-curve, crossing the down-stroke at base-line, and finishing at height of letter. The dimensions of the lower loop are the same as loop of small *g* and small *y*. *Extended* loop. *Three* spaces. *One* shade.

Analysis—Principles 1, 2, 2, 1.

Note.—The *z* is the only small loop letter in which the straight line or fifth principle is not used.

THE NUMERALS.

Nothing is more important to a business writer than the ability to execute *figures* properly. The qualities most desirable are: 1, legibility ; 2, conformity to space, position and style ; and 3, ease of execution and gracefulness of form. We place the characteristics in the order of their importance.

The correct examples given in copy-slip are the standard forms. For purely business purposes, they may be simplified by omitting some of the superfluous lines.

CHAPTER III.

THE CAPITALS EXPLAINED AND ANALYZED.

Before a letter can be correctly formed, some idea of its proportions, and the mode of combining its several parts, must exist in the mind. Hence the necessity of presenting true forms to the observation of those learning to write. As has been aptly expressed by one long skilled in the art of penmanship, "Make the mind master of the subject, and every servant of the house it lives in becomes obedient to the will."

We give in copy-slip VIII, a complete set of model capitals, and although they may be looked upon as standard letters, it is neither possible nor desirable for different persons to write precisely the same hand and style of capitals, we therefore introduce, throughout the copies, the three or four different styles approved of and practiced in book-keeping, record, and epistolary writing. This feature will not only do much towards cultivating good taste, but will aid young men and women in selecting and adopting a style suited to their wants, and best calculated to secure and preserve an individuality in their handwriting.

The capitals are formed from the five principles already explained and may be divided into three classes, viz.: the Stem letters, or those introduced by the compound curve called the Capital Stem, such as A, B, &c. ; the loop letters, such as Q, U, V, &c., and the oval letters, as O, E, &c. Capitals are uniformly *three times* the height of *minimum* small letters, and uniform with the extended loop letters. The width of no capital should ever equal its height. The base of every letter should equal or exceed the top in width, to present stability of appearance.

There are two ways of shading Capitals : upon the principal stroke, producing the plain style, and within the ovals producing the ornamental style. In the following analysis we give one entire alphabet and leave the other forms to the student to analyze himself.

The capitals to the right of the following explanations are not, in all instances, such as are best adapted to business. For the forms here explained see copy-slip VIII.

CAPITAL A (as in slip).

A The first part of Capital A is formed of the stem, made downward from top and slightly curved at top and bottom. Finish with an oval almost complete, occupying 1½ spaces from base line, throwing the shade wholly on the lower curve with a gradual increase and diminish. The second part is formed with downward stroke, light, and slightly curved. The finishing curve, known as the crossing of the letter, touches the second downward stroke just above the head-line, and, with an oval movement, crosses it at the centre of the lower space.

Analysis.—Principles 4, 1, 1, 1, 2.

CAPITAL B.

B The B at left does not correspond with description. See slip. The capital stem in this letter, though comprising the compound curve, as in Capital A, is both more curved at top and bottom, and stands more nearly perpendicular. Commence at top a little below height of letter and forming an oval turn at base, ascend with convex curve, maintaining a uniform distance from first stroke three spaces turning roundly at its height over the top of the stem, and entwining stem at centre with an upward pointing loop and finishing with a downward oval movement, dropping just below the base line ; and with the upward convex curve nearly joining the stem again at the middle, forming an almost perfect oval, with the lower curve of the stem running through its centre. Throw the shade entirely on the lower curve of the stem.

NOTE.—This letter constitutes one of the best exercises for practice that could possibly be given. It should invariably be made without lifting the pen. Carefully observe its proportions; and notice specially the fulness of the curve on the left of the stem.

Analysis.—Principles 4, 1, 2, 2, 1.

CAPITAL C (as in slip VIII).

C The movement of this letter is what is known as the direct oval, the second part of the letter being an exact oval of half the height of the letter. Commence with concave or compound curve, carried upward through three spaces, with a loop turn at top; the downward movement, being slightly curved, crosses the upward curve at the height of one space from base line, Forming a loop two spaces in length. Finish with direct oval of one half the height of the letter. Shade on centre of first downward stroke with gradual increase and diminution.

Analysis.—Principles 2, 1, 2, 1.

CAPITAL D.

Begins with capital stem, 1½ spaces high, which extends to the left on base line, turning and forming a small narrow loop running parallel with the base line, the movement resulting in a graceful compound curve, which yields to a full concave curve passing upward on the right of the stem, through three spaces, and extending over the top of the stem to the left, forming a direct oval which occupies 2½ spaces. The terminating oval is a perfect Capital O, shaded on first down-stroke. Observe the proportions of this letter carefully.

For a different style of this letter see slip X, word Delicate.

Analysis.—Principles 4, 1, 2, 1, 2, 1. *One* shade.

CAPITAL E.

The Capital E is formed of an oval curve one space in length, joined by a short descending loop to a regular Capital O, two spaces in length. The proportions of the letter and the position of the loop should be carefully preserved. The location of the shade in the example given is the best for ordinary work. Sometimes the first stroke in short oval is also shaded and looks well if properly done.

NOTE.—Before attempting the execution of this letter, the learner should practice upon the continuous O movement until he is able to form an ellipse with perfect ease.

Analysis.—Principles 1, 2, 1, 1, 2, 1.

CAPITAL F.

This letter is mostly formed of the Capital Stem, which is more curved both at top and bottom than in the Capital A. The top or *cap* of the letter is a graceful compound curve, running, in the main, horizontally, and joined to the stem by a small horizontal loop. This cap is sometimes thrown gracefully over the top of the stem, as above. The finishing curve which, joined with the stem at the base, unites in the formation of the terminating oval, passes across the centre of the stem, and ends with a slight upward movement; it is crossed by a short oblique line, making the characteristic cross of the letter. The finishing oval is one-half the height of the letter, and the shade is thrown wholly on the lower curve of the stem.

Analysis.—Principles 1, 5, 3, 4, 1, 5. *One shade.*

CAPITAL G.

This is one of the most substantial and graceful of the capitals, if well made. Its curves and proportions should be carefully noted. Commence on base-line with full concave curve running to the height of the letter ; turn into a loop at top, descending with a slight convex curve through two spaces, and, with an oval turn, rise again through three-fourths of a space, and end with a single curve capital stem, turning roundly at base, and terminating in a full oval 1½ spaces high, stopping just before touching the stem. The stem part should be properly shaded on lower curve.

Analysis.—Principles 2, 1, 2, 2, 1. *One shade.*

CAPITAL H.

The Capital H commences with the reversed oval movement, carried up 2½ spaces, dropping into a small loop-oval which may be lightly shaded on the down-stroke, and descending to base-line with a slight concave curve, thence returning on the left and forming a loop by crossing the down-stroke 1¼ spaces from base-line ; the upper movement continues, merging into a perfect Capital C, which forms the second and main part of the letter.

Analysis.—Principles 1, 2, 1, 2, 3, 1, 2, 1,

CAPITAL I.

The Capital I starts at a point just below the height of first space, with a convex curve carried well to the right, and turning into a small loop, continues up on the regular slant to the height of the letter—three spaces; at this point it unites with a regular capital stem, which passes down through the centre of the loop, terminating in the usual oval, with a small dot nearly touching the stem at its shaded point.

DIMENSIONS, ETC.—The first part or cap occupies the upper two spaces—the commencing small loop, a little more than half a space; the width of the final oval from base-line is one space and a half, which is two-thirds its length; the shade is wholly on the lower curve of the stem, heaviest at centre, and gradually diminishing each way.

Analysis.—Principles 1, 1, 4, 1.

Capital J.

The capital J starts at base line with convex curve, which turns into a round loop at the height of one space, thence passes on a more gradual curve to the height of three spaces from base-line ; here it unites with the stem, which, with slight compound curve, passes down through the centre of the small loop, five spaces, where, with a loop-turn, it unites with a convex curve, which, passing upward, crosses the stem at base-line, and continues to top of first space. The stem is shaded with gradual increase and diminution from base-line down.

Analysis.—Principles, 1, 1, 4, 1. *One shade.*

Capital K.

The Capital K commences at base-line with concave curve, which passes upward through 2½ spaces, where it joins a single-curve capital stem, having a moderate oval finish, and gradually shaded below the centre ; the second part of the letter commences at its height—three spaces from base-line—and with a compound curve (fourth principle) representing a small unshaded capital stem—strikes the main stem at its centre, entwining it with a small upward-pointing loop, thence passing with a slight compound curve (third principle) to the base-line, turning shortly on the line and passing up with a slight fourth-principle compound curve, carried through first space. The first upward curve divides the stem-oval a little to the right of its centre.

Analysis.—Principles, 2, 2, 1, 4, 3, 4. *One shade.*

Capital L.

The Capital L commences on base-line with concave curve, which passes upward three spaces, turning at the top into a loop formed on the left by the upper curve of the capital stem, which forms the body of the letter. The stem which is greatly curved at top and bottom, crosses the upstroke at its centre, coming down to base line with full, round, shaded curve, passing to left and returning with compound curve, which, crossing the down curve on base-line, forms a loop, running almost parallel with the line, and continues, ending with a concave curve passing one space high.

Analysis.—Principles 2, 4, 3. *One shade.*

Capital M.

The first and second parts of this letter is like capital A.; to the second stroke is joined at base line a returning upstroke, which is also a convex curve, inclining to the right; passing to height of letter (three spaces), this movement is joined to a downward stroke, which, turning roundly on base-line, merges into a small capital O, making the finish of the letter.

Analysis.—Principles 4, 1, 1, 1, 1, 2, 1. *Two shades.*

Capital N.

The Capital N differs from the Capital A in the additional finishing curve and the omission of the loop-crossing. The first part is the capital stem proper, with oval termination; the second part is a very slight convex curve brought from the top of the stem to the base-line on the regular slant; the finishing stroke joining the second part at base-line, runs up with convex curve, harmonizing in slant with first part, and ending at the distance of $1\frac{1}{2}$ spaces from base line.

Analysis.—Principles 4, 1, 1, 1. *One shade.*

Capital O.

The Capital O is a direct oval, occupying three spaces, the width being one-half the slanting length. Begin at top of third space, and with full convex curve, come down to base-line, turning roundly thereon and rising with a corresponding concave curve; turn at top just below the starting-point, and finish with a second downward convex curve running parallel with the first, and at a distance therefrom of one-fifth the width of the letter. The shade may be thrown on either of the down-strokes, and should be gradual, decreasing from the centre of the curve either way.

Analysis.—Principles 1, 2, 1. *One shade.*

Capital P.

This letter differs from the Capital B only in its termination, the last movement of B (reverse oval) being omitted, and the letter terminating in a dot across the centre of the stem where the loop of B touches. Observe the proportions of the letter; and especially the position, curvature and shade of the capital stem, and the space between the stem and the first upward curve.

Analysis.—Principles 4, 1, 2. *One* shade.

CAPITAL Q.

The main part of this letter is composed of the Capital Loop, and is, in effect, a double reverse-oval. Begin just at the second line, and with a full convex curve, pass to the height of the letter, turning at top with a full oval-turn and passing down with corresponding curvature to a point three-fourths of a space above the base-line ; with an oval tuin, pass upward again on a curve running parallel with first up-curve, at a distance therefrom of one-half the width of the oval loop ; cross the first down-curve at the same distance from the top of the letter, and pass downward on the right to base-line preserving the distance and harmony of curve ; a parallel loop is formed on the base-line corresponding in shape, size, and direction with that of capital D and capital L, and terminating in a compound curve which passes to the height of first space. The shade is thrown on second down-curve, heaviest in the centre and gradually decreases from the centre either way.

Analysis.—Principles 1, 2, 1, 2, 3. *One* shade.

CAPITAL R.

This letter varies from Capital B only in the final turn on the base-line. The form, proportions, and position in all other respects, are identical. Observe the upward-pointing of the small loop which entwines the stem at its centre. From thence, pass to base-line with a slight compound curve, turning to the right on base-line, and finishing with a slight compound curve at the height of one space.

Analysis.—Principles 4, 1, 2, 3, 4. *One* shade.

CAPITAL S.

A very beautiful as well as difficult letter. It is commenced like L, but instead of loop at base, closes with full convex curve, like A, N, &c.

Analysis.—Principles 1, 2, 4, 1, *One* shade.

CAPITAL T.

This letter differs from capital F only in the termination of the base-oval, the upper stroke of which in F crosses the stem constituting the characteristic of the letter. This style, combining the cap and the stem without lifting the pen, constitutes a standard form. These two parts may, however, be made separately, as explained in capital F. In this style, the cap is thrown gracefully over the top of the stem, without touching it. Practically, it is of little moment which is first formed, the stem or the cap.

Analysis.—Principles 4, 1, 1, 2, 3. *One shade.*

CAPITAL U.

The first part of Capital U is comprised of the capital loop movement turned roundly on the base-line ; the second part is connected by a continuous upward-moving concave curve at the height of two spaces, and is in form identical with the small *t* unshaded. The instructions as to the formation of the loop in capital Q will apply with equal force here.

Analysis.—Principles 1, 2, 1, 3, 2, 5 2. *One shade.*

CAPITAL V.

First part like U, the concave curve made upward from the base inclines more to the perpendicular and finishes with a graceful compound curve.

Analysis.—Principles 1, 2, 1, 3, 2. *One shade.*

CAPITAL W.

The first part of this letter differs but slightly from the Capital Q, difference being in inclination of down-stroke near the base-line. The parallel loop of Q on the base-line necessicates the greater inclination as the down-stroke reaches that point. At the same time the capital loop movement in W is more inclined than that in business M and N, where loop is used. This inclination is necessary to give the letter an easy and graceful position. The difference in slant of the downstrokes should be specially noted.

Analysis —Principles 1, 2, 1, 2, 2, 1, 1. *One shade.*

CAPITAL X.

The first part of Capital X is formed precisely like the first part of Capital W. The second part is a modified O, commencing at the height of the letter at a point where, by coming down on the regular slant, it just touches the first down-stroke at its centre. From this point, the movement diverges into a small capital O, of one half the height of the letter. When complete, the last half of the first down-stroke, and the first half of the second, have the appearance of a straight line *crossing* a compound curve.

Analysis.—Principles 1, 2, 1, 2, 1, 2, 1. *One shade.*

CAPITAL Y.

The first part of Capital Y is identical in form with the first part of Capital U and V. The second part joins the upward curve of the first part three-fourths of a space from the top, and passes two spaces below base-line on the proper slant of writing, turning roundly, and finishing with convex curve crossing downward stroke.

Analysis.—Principles 1, 2, 1, 2, 2, 5, 1. *One shade.*

CAPITAL Z.

The first or upper portion of Capital Z is identical in form and shade with the first part of Capital W. From the point of contact with the base line, a full convex curve passes upward crossing the main downstroke at the height of a half-space, forming a neat small loop; and continuing down two spaces below the base-line, united through a loop-turn with an upward convex curve, which crosses the down- stroke at the base-line, forming a loop, and ends at the height of first space.

Analysis.—Principles 1, 2, 1, 2, 1, 2, 1. *One shade.*

CHAPTER IV.

Lettering, Off-Hand Flourishing and Pen Drawing.

LETTERING.

German Text or Old English lettering are more available in ornamental work than any other style. The former is more frequently used on account of its conformity, through its curves, to ordinary writing, and the ease with which it is executed. We give, in our Ornamental Sheet, all the capital and small letters in German Text and Old English Alphabets. These letters should be written with a single stroke of a broad pointed pen, unless in instances where it is desirable to fill the body of the letters with ornamental shading, when the main strokes may be outlined with an ordinary steel pen. The best pen for this kind of lettering is made from the quill of a turkey, the nib being made broad to correspond with the width of the main down-strokes. A little careful practice will enable a person of ordinary skill to form both German Text and Old English with a precision and effect that is really astonishing.

OFF-HAND FLOURISHING.

Off-hand flourishing is more generally appreciated by lovers of artistic work than any other department of penmanship. We have submitted a variety of models in this department. The flourishes should be practiced first, in the order of their numbers, and after the position of pen holding as illustrated in sketch of hand, and an accuracy and freedom of stroke are obtained, they may be blended into almost any form.

POSITION OF HAND AND PEN.

Hold the pen between the thumb and second finger, the first finger being thrown well up to steady the pen, press the thumb carefully on the lower part of the holder, just above the pen, which will enable you to regulate the shading without difficulty. The third and fourth fingers should be thrown a little back and raised clear of the paper when making long lines, but when making short lines and fine shading the small finger may rest on the paper.

Keep the pen square on the paper, touching equally on each nib, and make the strokes horizontally from left to right, shifting the paper to suit the direction you wish the curves to take. A good off-hand penman keeps the working sheet separate from the others and constantly shifts it about, but does not change the position of the pen or the direction of the curves, unless they are continuous, when they are made in various directions.

Make all the large bold curves and heavy shades first; the fine ornamentation and shading should be done afterward by going over the work slowly and carefully, using the finger-rest.

A little practice, holding the pen as explained above, and illustrated in Ornamental Sheet, will convince you that flourishing is not the wonderful feat it may appear to be, to those who have tried it by holding the pen in the ordinary way.

We have given two specimens of Pen-Drawing which will answer as an exercise for those who wish to practice this art. This Ornamental Sheet was executed with a pen and reproduced by the process of Photo-Lithography. They are photographed on stone, therefore, every line, dot and imperfection of the original copy is reproduced in this fac simile.

ONTARIO COMMERCIAL COLLEGE, BELLEVILLE, ONT.
A MODEL BUSINESS SCHOOL,

Where the course of study is directly adapted to the exigencies of the age and times :—short, practical, useful and reasonable;

Training Young Men, Boys, and Middle-Aged Men in the shortest possible time, and at the least expense, for active successful business life; teaching them how to transact business for themselves, how to manage business for others, and how to become useful, enterprising citizens.

The subjects taught are just such as every Merchant, Farmer, Mechanic, and Professional Man requires in transacting the affairs of every-day life, and embrace the following:—

Book-Keeping as applied to every department of business, Penmanship, Arithmetic, Correspondence, Practical Grammar, Commercial Geography, Spelling, Telegraphing, Mechanical and Architectural Drawing, Phonography, &c.

The generality of our young men who wish to fit themselves for business, become Accountants or learn a trade, have neither time nor money to expend in obtaining a smattering of Latin and Greek, or on ages past and gone, and should therefore devote their time and attention to the acquisition of the branches adapted to the particular business they intend to pursue. Our sole time and attention is devoted to the teaching of such subjects and the result of our labors for the past seven years is shown by the hundreds of our graduates who are either conducting a successful business for themselves or filling positions as Accountants, Telegraph Operators, or Salesmen at salaries ranging from $500 to $2,000 per annum.

☞ This is the most extensive and best patronized Business School in Canada, and the only one *where the course of training is practical instead of theoretical,* where the time of the student is devoted to only such subjects as are required to prepare him for transacting the business of every-day life, where students act as *Buyers, Sellers, Traders, Bankers, and Book-Keepers* in actual business operations, where the bank bills and merchandise are actually used and have a real value and where the transactions are as "bona fide" as in any real business.

To the hundreds of parents whose greatest concern is the prosperity of their sons, just starting in active life, and to the young and middle aged men of the country seeking a successful start in business, is presented the claims of this institution.

The instructors in the different departments are the best that can be procured. We obtained first prizes in all departments of penmanship, viz.: Business Hand, Ornamental Penmanship, and Card Writing, at the Provincial Exhibition, and our specimens were selected by the Government Commissioners to send to the Centennial Exhibition at Philadelphia, as specimens of Canadian pen art.

GENERAL INFORMATION IN REGARD TO "ONTARIO COMMERCIAL COLLEGE."

Its Character.—It is a *live, practical common-sense school,* suited to the wants of the times. It is conducted by *able* and *competent teachers.* It is endorsed by the Press, by prominent Business Men, by Educators, and by those who have been the recipients of its teachings.

Course of Study.—The course of study, is short, practical, useful and is just what every man needs, and what every successful man uses, no matter what his calling or profession may be. (See description of course, page 38.)

Time of Entering.—We have no vacations and consequently no fixed time for entering. Students can enter any week-day during the year with equal advantage, but now is always the best time to prepare for the work of life.

Necessary Qualifications.—An ordinary common school education constitutes a sufficient preparation for entering the college, and any special deficiency in this, if not too great, can be remedied in our course. There are no examinations at the time of commencing.

Time Required —The time required to complete the course depends entirely on the previous advancement, ability and application of the student.

Some graduate in three months, while others require six. The average time is about four months.

Classification.—We have sufficient classification to secure the best results from oral instruction, black-board illustrations, &c., without retarding or unduly advancing individual students.

Individual Instruction,—Each student will receive such individual instruction as will best advance him in his studies.

Examinations.—Careful and thorough examinations are held, and no student can be advanced from one department to another until he gives satisfactory evidence that he understands well what he has passed over.

Books & Stationery.—The total cost of Stationery, including Text Books, Blank Books, Notes, Checks, Bills, Paper, Pens, Ink, Envelopes, &c., from $8 to $10.

Rules.—Quiet, orderly deportment and strict attention to business, is a general regulation. A list of special rules is furnished to students.

Discipline.—The school rooms are sacred to the purposes of instruction, and are so held absolutely, In the furtherance of this purpose the teachers will employ all necessary authority. Students who cannot submit to the regulations are respectfully constrained to vacate their seats in favor of those who can.

School Hours.—Regular hours of study and recitation are from 9 to 12 A. M. and from 1:30 to 4 P. M., five days of the week.

Attendance.—Unless specially arranged for, students are expected to be in regular attendance during these hours.

Diplomas.—Our diplomas were engraved specially for this institution, and are the most beautiful granted by any Business College in Canada. Diplomas are granted only to those who complete the Business, or Special Penmanship Course and pass thorough examinations.

INTERIOR VIEW OF BUSINESS DEPARTMENT.

DESCRIPTION OF OUR COURSE OF STUDY.

Our course of study is *comprehensive,* and adapted not only to such as have enjoyed the best educational advantages, but also to those whose education is deficient, from want or neglect of early opportunity, or other cause.

To those who desire to engage in agricultural pursuits, it gives a practical knowledge, and experience in business, which enables them to meet the shrewd business man with a confidence in their own ability, that secures them from imposition and fraud.

It gives the mechanic an opportunity to take a front rank, by reason of superior ability to transact with correctness the business of his calling.

Those engaged in mercantile life will receive that which is invaluable to them in the safety and despatch with which they will be able to conduct their own business and that of others.

And to that large class who are uncertain what course to pursue, it is not only the best stepping-stone to lucrative and permanent business of their own, but also a ready means of commanding regular employment.

The following synopsis will give an idea of the prescribed course of study in the different departments :

The business course embraces three departments, viz. : Theoretical Junior, Theoretical Senior, and Actual Business Departments.

Our system of initiation is peculiar to this institution, and with our daily lectures and blackboard illustrations, does away wi*h the long days and hours of working and groping in the dark, that most students experience when initiated by the system established in the days of fogyism.

In the Theoretical Department the elementary principles which are to guide the student through this comprehensive course are taught. Here the rudiments of Penmanship, the principles of accounts, the art of correspondence, the use and application of arithmetic in all the practical concerns of life, and the forms and use of business paper, such as Notes, Drafts, Checks, Bills of Exchange, Receipts, Orders, Due Bills, &c., &c. ; are so unfolded and elucidated that the dullest perception will readily understand and appreciate them.

After a thorough drill and initiation, the student opens, writes up and closes different sets of books, which, with particular forms and illustrations, adapted to every kind of business, as taken from the first business houses, and sanctioned by the best accountants and bookkeepers of the country, give him an extended knowledge.

The course of study in this Department embraces duties in somewhat the following order :

1st. Exercises in Penmanship, giving the correct position, and use of the Muscular Movement, in order to become a bold rapid business writer.

2nd. Studying the language of trade, and the theory of accounts.

3rd. Learning by the most simple and progressive process the principles of Debit and Credit, the classification of accounts, the process of making out trial balances, statements, etc.

4th. Exercises in different kinds of ruling, and learning to make neat and cleanly cut figures.

5th. Lectures on business practice, or mercantile economy and the general management of business.

6th. The most approved and rapid method of working the Simple Rules of Arithmetic, Reduction, Fractions, Percentage and Interest.

7th. Exercises on Ledger Headings.

8th. Domestic and foreign correspondence, studying the forms and use of business paper, learning how to stamp notes drafts, &c.

9th. Studying the use of Auxiliary Books as well as the Day Book, Journal and Ledger.

10th. Balancing books, adjusting partnership settlements, etc.

When all the work assigned in this department is correctly performed and satisfactory examinations passed, the student is promoted to the

Senior Theoretical Department.

He being now prepared, more difficult work is presented,—work that will give him a wide field for thought and effort. Here is where his latent energies are brought out, and the knowledge acquired in the previous part of the course, tested in a field of labor that calls forth the highest order of executive skill, from the simplest forms of copartnership to the most advanced and intricate exercises to be met with in any business :

1st. The introduction and use of the different auxiliary books.

2nd. Different forms of keeping books, in order that the transactions may be posted in totals, thereby abbreviating the work.

3rd. Transactions representing the different changes that occur in business.

4th. Advanced exercises in Arithmetic, such as Equation of payments, Equation of Accounts, General Average, etc.

5th. Lectures on Penmanship, and advanced exercises therein daily.

6th. Forwarding and Commission Business.

This part of the course is carefully and critically watched, no student being permitted to pass from one step to another without a thorough and satisfactory examination.

After giving sufficient evidence of a thorough knowledge of the priciples and practice of business, the student is promoted to the

Actual Business Department.

Having pursued his studies thus far with special reference to the exigencies of a business life, he now engages in those pursuits which will test the value of his instruction. Here he is assigned his official desk, and furnished with a capital, consisting of Cash, Real Estate, Merchandise, &c., corresponding with the business in which he is to engage, and opens books accordingly. He rents a store, commences business, buys and sells merchandise, real estate, stocks, &c., makes deposits in the bank, gives and receives checks, receipts, orders, notes, acceptances, drafts, account sales, etc. ; holds correspondence with different firms through the post-office, computes all interest, discount, and other calculations in connection with his business trans actions, and finally balances his books weekly.

He commences as sole proprietor, but admits a new partner at the beginning of every set, thereby augmenting his capital, and acquiring practical experience in effecting partnership settlements, bankrupt settlements, etc.

Having had sufficient practice in this direction, and passed the requisite examinations successfully, the student is now admitted to the

Graduating Department or Offices.

He first enters the Merchants Emporium, which represents a large wholesale establishment, and is furnished with the necessary books, to divide the labor among the different book-keepers. This is the department whence all goods supplied to students on entering the Actual Business Course emanate. He first enters as a clerk, and is promoted step by step, until he becomes acquainted with the whole routine of this miniature establishment, after which he becomes over-seer or general manager.

He now feels his responsibility, and acquires a degree of facility and confidence in actual business operations, such as could not be acquired by theoretical training. From this position he passes into the

COLLEGE BANK,

which is an actual bank of deposit, discount and circulation, pro-vided with its own bills, checks, notes, &c., furnished with a full set of books, and the business done with as much accuracy and dexterity as in a regular banking establishment.

The above synopsis is sufficient to show the superiority of our sys-tem of instruction. It makes the pupil practically acquainted with every variety of business trnsactions, from the simple details of a country store, to the more complicated operations of extensive mer-cantile and banking establishments. It will also be observed that this course gives the student a practical knowledge of Mathematics, Spelling, Composition, Grammar, and the English branches generally, that cannot be obtained so readily in any other way.

The above course of study is arranged especially for that class of

42

persons, both young men and boys, and men of middle age, who desire to qualify themselves in the shortest possible time, and at the least expense, to fill successfully, positions as book-keepers and accountants, or to engage in actual business of any kind.

RATES OF TUITION.

NOTE.—Owing to the extensive patronage we receive from all parts of the country we are enabled to place our rates of tuition $25 less than city Commercial Colleges, which have but a local patronage ; this, with the difference in the price of good boarding accommodation, for four months, makes the total expense of a student Fifty Dollars less than at the smaller Institutions, that have less facilities and advantages.

☞ *The total expense of Tuition, Board and Stationery for four months* (in which time the Business course is completed) *is from $85 to $100, as follows :*

Scholarship for the full course, to be, completed at the option of the student, including Book-Keeping as applied to Wholesale and Retail Merchandising, Manufacturing, Banking, Settlement of Estates, Farming, Railroading, Steamboating, &c , Penmanship, Arithmetic, Business Correspondence, Commercial Law, Practical Grammar, Spelling, Commercial Geography, Business Paper, &c., &c,, $40.

When two enter from the same place at the same time a deduction of $3 is made from each scholarship. A deduction of $5 is made from each scholarship when three enter from the same place at the same time.

When a club of four enter from the same place, at the same time a deduction of $5 will be made from each scholarship, and $5 extra to the person getting up the club.

This arrangement is made to reduce the terms to families who have several to send, and also that those who spend their time inducing others to accompany them, may be remunerated for the same.

Those who thoroughly qualify themselves will be assisted in procuring business situations. We have a great many applications for young men of the right stamp.

The tuition fee must be payed on the day of entrance.

BOARD

Is from $2.50 to $3.00 per week, according to place, in private families. Some students hire rooms and board themselves for half this price.

BOOKS AND STATIONERY.

The total cost of Stationery, including Text Books, Blank Books, Notes, Checks, Bills, Paper, Pens, Ink, Envelopes, &c., is from $8 to $10 and is purchased by the student from time to time as required.

☞ There are no extra or other expenses in the Business course than those herein mentioned.

TO PARENTS AND GUARDIANS.

That parents and others may understand the actual cost of a Business course, and not be led astray by misrepresentations made by young men who may expend money for unnecessary purposes, we desire it understood that *One Hundred Dollars* covers the entire expenses of a full course. This is all that is absolutely necessary to be expended by any young man during his attendance, and those who take cheaper boarding accommodation reduce the amount.

EXPENSES OF A FULL COURSE.
(Including Everything.)

Life Scholarship	$40 00
Stationery	10 00
Board for 16 weeks at $3	48 00
Extras	2 00
Total	$100 00

The above sum is given as the total amount necessary for a thorough course of Commercial Study at this institution, though some students go through a course for from $65 to $75. That there may be *no misunderstanding* on this subject, the Principal will, if desired by the parent or guardian, pay the expenses of any student, as above described for the sum of $100. In such cases, monthly statements of expenditures are rendered.

Telegraph Department.

Instructions Theoretically and Practically, with use of both Paper and Sound Instruments, and lectures on the minutæ of office business:

Life Scholarship to students in the Commercial Department	$20.00
To all others	25.00

Phonography, (Evening Sessions.)

Term of threee months	$5.00

Mechanical Department (Evening Sessions.)

Instructions in Mechanical and Architectural Drawing, Constructive Geometry, &c.

Term of four months... $5.00

Ornamental Penmanship Department.

This Department is designed for the accommodation of those who wish to give more than ordinary attention to Penmanship and Drawing, and is especially adapted to the preparation of those wishing to become master penmen or to qualify themselves to teach the art in all its various branches.

The course embraces Business and Epistolary Writing, Off-hand Flourishing, every imaginary style of Plain and Ornamental Lettering, including German Text, Italic, Old English, ROMAN, RUSTIC and other Lettering, Card Writing, both plain and ornamental, Fine Pen Shading, Pen and Pencil Pictures, Preparing Specimens for Framing, &c. &c., and is systematically arranged, the student taking up principles, letters, words, sentences, and the different varieties of Pen Work in regular order.

TIME.

The time required to graduate, in this department, is from six weeks to three months, depending upon how comprehensive a course is desired.

TERMS OF TUITION.

Scholarship, Special Course, (time unlimited,)................$30
Same to students in Business Course,........................ 20

Why Young Men Prefer Attending Ontario Business College.

1. It is universally acknowledged to be the leading Business College in Canada.

2. It is under the management of practical and experienced men, assisted by able teachers, who give their entire time and attention to the interests of the school and its students.

3. Students are here exempt from the evil temptations that, on every side, beset them in a large city.

4. The expense of completing a course here is very small as compared with that of large cities ; board, tuition, and other expenses being from one-half to one-third less.

5. Its course of instruction is comprehensive and thorough and is practically adapted to the wants of the times.

6. It has the confidence and hearty support of business men, and its graduates are in demand.

7. It has one of the best penmen in the land, who gives thorough instruction, in Penmanship, daily to the school.

8. The diplomas are good recommendations of ability to perform the duties of an accountant.

9. It has commodious, well ventilated and well furnished rooms, properly fitted for actual business prretice.

10. Students have the privilege of attending the largest, the most thorough and practical, and the best patronized business school in Canada, at a much less outlay than that of the small local colleges in cities.

TESTIMONIALS.

We place before the reader, with pleasure, the following testimonials from graduates and prominent business men, selected from many more in our possession, which we are compelled to omit for want of space.

FROM STUDENTS WHILE IN ATTENDANCE.

We, the undersigned students, now in attendance, and about completing our course at Ontario Commercial College, beg to return our sincere thanks to the Principal and Teachers for their untiring energy and labor bestowed upon us during our connection with the Institution. We also take pleasure in recommending this College to all who desire to obtain a thorough and practical business education. We speak from experience, and can confidently say, that this school is in every particular what it is represented to be. It is perfect in all its appointments, systematic and thorough in its course of instruction, which is of the most practical character, and cannot fail to be eminently useful to all its students. We believe it is the best institution of the kind in this country, and shall ever look back to the time we have so pleasantly and profitably spent in it with feelings of gratitude and pleasure, and our best wishes will always remain with Messrs. S. G. Beatty & Co., for the prosperity their College so richly deserves.

W. H. McGANNON,
Prescott, Ont.

GEO. E. REID,
Portage du Fort, Que.

GEO T. FULFORD,
Brockville, Ont.

CHAS. F. HALL,
Napanee, Ont.

S. MITCHELL,
Peterboro, Ont.

A. RICKEY,
Mill Haven, Ont.

W. W. POPE,
Fitchburg, Mass.

A. J. COUCH,
Montreal, Que.

JOSIAH BENSON,
Picton, Ont.

E. C. PLANE,
Port Hope, Ont.

MARTIN SEELEY,
Stirling, Ont.

J. H. ROWLAN,
Guelph, Ont.

JOHN WILSON,
Aberdeen, Scotland.

H. YOUNG,
Mallorytown, Ont.

GEO. L. JOHNSON,
Lansdowne, Ont.

W. O. ALLEN,
Cobden, Ont.

GEO. MURPHY,
Clarendon, Que.

N. V. DUDLEY,
Colborne, Ont.

A. ESMOND,
Thurlow, Ont.

T. S. SPAFFORD,
Belleville, Ont.

A. C. PARKS,
Napanee, Ont.

J. W. BROOKS,
Stirling, Ont.

H. CAMPBELL,
Melrose, Ont.

R. S. Davy,
Detroit, Mich.

Committee representing students in Attendance.

The above, presented to the Principal and Teachers by the Students after a farewell address, from one who was about to take leave of us, shows the appreciation in which the College is held by those attending it.

FROM OUR TOWNSMEN.

S. G. BEATTY & Co.,

DEAR SIRS,—We, the undersigned, citizens of Belleville, appreciating your labors in behalf of practical, useful education, and in building up in our midst an institution of learning of such magnitude and importance as your Business College, congratulate you on the high character it has both at home and abroad.

We have watched your Institution from its small commencement until it has grown to its present large dimensions, and know of none more thorough and practical, affording, as it does, to our youths facilities for preparing for active successful life.

We recognise in the business principles it teaches, the practical method it inculcates, and the experience it secures to the student, a general benefaction, which should commend it to those who have sons to educate, and to young men whatever their future calling in life is to be.

Hon. Robert Read, Senator.	J. & W. Sutherland, Dry Goods.
Hon. Billa Flint, "	Robertson & Empey, "
M. Bowell, M. P.	Nathan Jones, "
James Brown, M. P.	Thos. Ritchie, "
G. E. Henderson, Mayor.	J. J. Harrison, Stationery.
A. F. Wood, Warden.	L. W. Yeomans, & Co., Drugs.
S. Young, Manager R. C. Bank.	Haines & Lockett, Boots & Shoes.
Foster & Barber, Dry Goods.	Conger Bros., Groceries.
J. W. Dunnett, "	Ontario Publishing Co.,
G. C. Holton & Co., "	And one hundred others.

S. G. Beatty & Co.,

Gentlemen,—It gives me great pleasure to add my testimony to that of many others of your graduates in favor of your Business College.

Having had considerable experience as a teacher, and five years' practice as a book-keeper, previous to entering your Institution, I consider myself competent to judge of the efficiency and practicability of your course, and must recommend it in the highest terms, to those who desire a thorough and diversified system of business training, that will prepare them to keep books of any kind.

Thanking you for recommending me to a position, I remain yours very truly,

R. D. ANGLIN,
(H. M. Customs, Kingston.)

Having enjoyed frequent opportunities of examining specimens of the penmanship of Mr. S. G. Beatty, and also of observing the progress made by pupils under his instruction, it affords me much pleasure to testify to his eminent qualifications to teach this and the other branches of a sound commercial education.

REV. SEPTIMUS JONES, M. A.,
Toronto.

Messrs S. G. Beatty & Co., Commercial College, Belleville,

I have never regretted the day I resolved to abandon school teaching and prepare myself for business.

Immediately after graduating at your institution, I secured a lucrative and pleasant situation here as accountant.

The thoroughness of your instruction gave me a confidence that enabled me to enter upon my duties without fear of dissatisfaction to my employers.

I have learned from experience that your system is of the most practical nature, and would recommend all who desire to become expert and scientific accountants to attend the Commercial College at Belleville.

Your former student,

J. R. MORAN, Montreal.

———

Mr. S. G. Beatty, Commercial College, Belleville, Ont.

Dear Sir,—After watching your mode of teaching for many years past, it gives me much pleasure to add this, my opinion of you, to the many testimonials you have so worthily received from others.

I therefore say that, in the art of governing pupils and imparting to them instruction, but few of your equals have ever come under my observation.

Further, I may now say that I am well satisfied with the Business instruction which my son, who is now in the Merchant's Bank received under your tuition,

THOMAS WILLS, M. P. P.,

Belleville.

———

Messrs. S. G. Beatty & Co., Commercial College.

Dear Sirs,—I have much pleasure in acknowledging the great progress made by my son while under your tuition, for four months during last winter. His advancement in writing, arithmetic, bookkeeping, &c., was remarkably good, and speaks volumes for the system you have adopted in instructing those under your care. I consider the establishment of your College of the greatest benefit to the country. With many thanks for your attention to my son.

I am your most obedient servant,

J. A. PONTON,

Registrar Hastings Co.

49

CROWN TIMBER OFFICE, Belleville, Ont.

MESSRS. S. G. BEATTY & Co.,

GENTLEMEN,—I feel much pleased with the progress made by my four children while attending your Institution. Your system is both thorough and practical, and I believe every young man should avail himself of the advantages your College offers, no matter what his future occupation may be.

Yours, &c,,

J. F. WAY,
Agent for Ontario Territory.

———

CROWN OFFICE, BELLEVILLE.

MESSRS. S. G. BEATTY & Co.,

MY DEAR SIRS,—I have great pleasure in recommending you to the public, and am glad you meet with that success your under-taking deserves.

As I can speak from a *personal knowledge* of your system, I feel certain all will be pleased and satisfied who give you a trial.

I am, Sirs, yours truly,

A. G. NORTHRUP.

.